THE GRANARY

Books by Kim R. Stafford

A Gypsy's History of the World
Braided Apart (with William E. Stafford)
The Granary

THE GRANARY

poems by

Kim R. Stafford

Carnegie-Mellon University Press
Pittsburgh 1982
Feffer and Simons, Inc., London

ACKNOWLEDGMENTS

Thanks to the editors of the following publications where some of these poems first appeared: *Carolina Quarterly, Clearwater Journal, CutBank, GiltEdge, Greenfield Review, The Hudson Review, Kansas Quarterly, The Malahat Review, Mid-American Review, Poetry Northwest, The Small Farm, South Carolina Review, Three Rivers Poetry Journal,* and *The Virgina Quarterly Review.*

"The Lighthouse" first appeared in *The Hudson Review.*

The epigraph on page 21 is from an Eskimo poem translated by Jerome Rothenberg and Knud Rasmussen in *Shaking the Pumpkin* (Garden City: Doubleday: 1972).

The publication of this book is supported by grants from the National Endowment for the Arts in Washington, D.C., a Federal agency, and from the Pennsylvania Council on the Arts.

Library of Congress Catalog Card Number 81-69799
ISBN 0-915604-64-7
ISBN 0-915604-65-5 pbk.

Printed and bound in the United States of America
First Edition

CONTENTS

*Deep in the granary
all seeds of wheat
are one in spirit.*

– dream

RAIN IN THE MOUNTAINS

Rain comes to earth,
an owl to a mouse in the grass;
the wind enters a budding tree;
a man comes to a woman—
it is the magnetism
of all things.

Brightest leaves fall to water;
water coheres, ice blooms;
the leaves shatter from themselves
at the tiny mouth of the root.

Within the body the body of water
is pulled by the moon, the self drawn
to another integrity, called away,
delight departing, sorrow ebbing
into the sway of a further brilliance.

Snow comes to earth,
a woman to a man—
it is the magnetism
of all things.

THE VINE

Often weathered by winter's mind
on a hill alone a hollow snag
lifts a branch, the last alive,
fragile skyward. Fire-skein flickers,
lightning lunges, limbs wither,
trunk melts, a tangle of coal;
the wheel of flame whirls and opens,
fireball blossoms, the boughs blaze
glowing with leaves grafted to ash.
A small seed stumbles out,
sheds the husk, shorn by fire.
By nudge and thrust the thicket shakes.
A lone stem stiffens green,
trunk and limb leaf-softened,
the bud breaks, bare heart-pocket
wet and rare, a winter bloom.

When dew is done, dawn begins.
Then the wind winding slow
shall inward after its own beginning–
that is travel, target within;
from the twisted wreck of a ruined tree
hollowed by fire, frost-stung
I was born, buried deep,
earth-blessed, eager to begin.
But light was still, the language I knew;
a clench of ice closed the ground.
Snow-sisters, sleet-brothers
scattered the field furrow by furrow,

hunger-farm harrowed by wind,
cold harvest, hail's granary,
festival of the lost. Lame and numbed
by winter's way, awake I waited.
From a cave I rose, quivered and entered
air through a crown of crumbled earth,
split and flinched from my first self
into lace that penetrates. Limbs that climb
pierced the dark, dirt dividing
from the leaf-journey, jewels of dew
twitching and turning toward the light,
the shining hill shadow-held,
the sun-road steep, slant of moon
curving over all colors of earth,
the bird-wheel backed by dusk,
the moment of rest. Remember now
how a star falls, a flash of treasure
swelling full, then swallowed by the dark.

Gypsy cocklebur, captive wanderer
falls in the grass, gone to ground,
housed under heaven. At home within
its little world, a lone bloom
lifts open in the lean wind
of late winter, alive so early,
marooned on earth, in the ring of cold
ever hopeful, eager to begin.

A SERMON ON EVE

'You know Eve's mother was a man,'
he said, 'and she one bone too many
in his side when he lay numb
and lazy in the summer grass alone?
Down fell the sun on that only
naked man, and stirred within him
then; he slept, and she rose
lovely from the bone, parted
from him for a bride, fair,
full-grown, filled with bewilderment
to be conceived and shaped and so
delivered into flesh. And there
old Adam lay still dreaming on,
stretched foolish, awkward at her feet,
helpless in sleep and solitude, bare
as stone but warm and breathing
like a wave. Sisters and brothers,
when his eyes bloomed wide, and he
looked up for her dark form
against the sun, the plain radiance
of light and shape, of hair
where it glimmered, caused
his mouth to open as he lay
bound within her swaying shadow
of the grass. She looked upon him,
saw the careless sprawl of his limbs
gather, afraid and separate, chilled
by her departure from within

his body's chamber. Her heart was
clenched against returning there—
the air was warm; she stirred, no
longer rooted to him, turned away
yet lingered by. My children, this
is the beginning—how each created thing
knows itself, a single spinning in delight
that then is woven to the world again
and dwells within the garden. Wind
embraced the willow there, and Eve's hair
billowed, and her arms were lifted
in a flame of praise. Old Adam, husk
from which she came, lay stilled
by wonder in the grass, withered
like us all when God the midwife's
sudden hands draw forth and shape
for other purposes the kindled spirit
from our frame that labors at its loss
but then lies quiet and content. Good
people, Eve bowed and gave him breath
again. Peace to you all. Amen.'

RED CLOUD

Right after the tornado
they drove down the road
to Evelyn's farm: the barn
planks scattered over the field,
the house gone simply–only
the floor, the sewing machine
standing.

There was Evelyn's dress,
thin in the splintered
branches of the cottonwood
where she went through
spinning into the sky,
and then her child
set somehow down
crying in a furrow
halfway to the river.

TAKING ANNA HOME

There was a place on the map
I wanted to be, to be
out in my white coat
where the streets carry a name
for miles, and rain trembles down
where you are waiting for it,
and a streetlight holds a place
between all the dark addresses
for a stranger to be resting.
I wanted to be cold and still
to live, to be hungry and
still to live, to be often alone
in search of this, to be
content, not by certain comforts
added to life, but by life itself.
Keep going this way–I will know it
when we find it.

THE YEW

A way of speaking:
the field brightened
in one syllable, low
clamor of the bees,
rain clear yet visible,
small flowers intent
at the soft core of seed.

The fir shall be straight,
the yew curve and tangle
alone. Water shall receive
what falls, wind only happen
by leaving home, the moon
rising, the tide returning.
Stand apart. Listen.

Awake, asleep,
we are finished, we are
not yet made. A traveler
passes through our lives
like a season. The storm
ends this way: a path
of dew.

Where fog occurs
by dawn the forgotten
red berry sweet with pitch,
green limbs, red bark,
spry wood, red heart hold
firm in earth for good:
living talisman of change.

Deep inside the yew
within the dark wood
at the central knot
where every limb
joins the others, you
are a wheel spun from light:
the eye, the yew, the bee.

THE BONES

Just before sleep I saw the bones
dancing together, woman and man
never touching, a cushion of air
like flesh between, the bones
white and graceful, a reptilian
tenderness for all the brittle
fabric of their being;
and from the woman
a child came out
through the bones
from the nothing at the belly
through the hip-door
eyes open, a face and fingers
reaching, and the father's
bones reaching out to take it
into the world.

KINDLING

Was it the long valley of my coat
thrown over the bed, or the ragged shoes
waiting by the door to be let out
on their own?

Inside me walked another life,
passive for a time in the wooden
embrace of muscle and gravity,
forgiving for a time the reluctance
of hand, tongue, and eye.
For time would begin
when the air cleared, light
brushed aside, and only
the naked gestures of the hands
leaving the hands behind
set out.

Where I stood
like thistledown when the wind beckons
shed from the body I whirled
out the bone roof in a gown of fire
loving that haggard scaffold
nameless in the doorway.

LA LLORONA

When I went walking by the water early
and mist unfurled the trees before me
and the river was only a sound,
the ground held steady under my feet
until I saw a woman
wavering through the grass, her green
bundle bound in a lace—

    llorona, ay qué llorona.

She brought her bundle to the water,
loosed the white cord as one
to another, woman to man,
man to woman. Then
the wrapping of leaves dropped away.
Mist held the trees, and the woman
the pale core of her bundle—

    llorona, ay qué llorona.

'Madre de oscuridad, madre
de cielo, madre de tierra,
madre de la soledad . . . '
She saw me in the leaves
and rose as if her bones
wore only a song;
the mist between us cleared—
    llorona, ay qué llorona.

She held out her child, a blur
grown small as if receding;

the woman closed her eyes.
I stumbled toward her
in a human way–all I knew.
She parted the bright leaves where
wind made a path in the willows–

    llorona, ay qué llorona.

My feet found the hard path again; but
still, since then, in the rain or dark
I've seen her face crumple like a flame
beckoning from the old world where I
lost my way by the water early
and mist unfurled the trees before me
and the river was only a sound.

PARABLE OF GROWING OLD

. . . and all women who refused to be
tattooed, not caring to suffer a little
to become beautiful.
>   —Eskimo description of hell

I

Grandfather, lost in the snow at night
without a proper coat, began to burn
everything he had, hoping to be found:
his only match struck first the strands
from his map torn away, flickering ribbon
hand to hand, then the dollars in his
pocket became a chain of fire—
George, Abraham, Alexander, Benjamin—
then page by page the addresses
of relatives, friends, good people
melted into the flame that lit
his face, eyes glittering at the last
leave-taking on the mountain, no
friend, tree, or sound for miles,
and at the end a photograph—
face withering, the eyes
without change in the long
blossoming of age
ringed by fire in his hands.

II

It happened this way
in the dream of a woman
wakened by fear to see the window

salted by stars, a kind of snow
that falls without an earth to find.
She rose from his bed
to find in the mirror such a
wrinkle of light on face, on hand,
and him behind her shoulder,
horizontal, calm.

III

This moment passes from one to another:
I know her only in the photograph,
the doorway, summer afternoon, her form
softened by the pale fire of all things old.
But sometimes in the evening, when I
leave the others to wash, I see her
that way in the glass–I a man, and young–
how gently she blooms into my face
in the dim light.

THE ROCKING CHAIR

In the earthquake the rocking chair,
patient so long, begins to move.

In the earthquake, people have no time
for the rocking chair, their shadows
scuttling across the floor, while
the rocking chair takes it easy,
leans back, lets it happen:

the comb thrown down, the dishes
chattering, the mirror flickering
through the air, and birds
leaving the world for good.
But the rocking chair stays
in touch, thoughtful, calm—
a little squeak at the joints
like every afternoon.

When the yard yawns wide, the house
lurching from its crumbling foundation,
and everyone like moles stumbling
suddenly into the daylight, no one
notices the sun crossing the floor
faster than most days,
except the rocking chair
on its smiling feet
dancing alone
in a corner.

THE POWER THAT SOFTENS ICE

First I was a moth that fluttered
clumsily over the field, wings
too small for my human body,
the crowd with its torches below
like wheat leaning after me.

Then on the mountain I was
the core of fire. Swaying,
the flame took splintered
boards from my hands.
The crowd turned me to wind;

utterly pliant in
filament of arm and leg
I drifted through the shaggy trees.
Then, I was the power that
softens ice, takes it out by hand

from a weathered boat. Crystals
of clear light rattled away
downstream. Then two women came
knee-deep in the cold; their hands,
the soft hinges of butterflies,

turned me to water. I was
eye-level with the current
that traveled between trees.
I knew a waterfall just ahead
but was not afraid. I was water.

I could survive any shattering.

SHORT STORY

Sometimes, reading late
and the others are asleep,
simple words like *rug,*
bright, window, late, road
have made a dim room by itself
way out in Wyoming; and then
work, month, injury, fear
bring the husband home, to
the drive, into the hall,
while the woman with *fist,*
cold, whisper, nest, fool
waits in bed, pretending
to be awake, the lamp burning,
in her damp hands a magazine
trembling–*years, boot, switch, door,*
and you, reading, fall
into your own life
happy and afraid
closing the book.

INHERITANCE AT WHEATLAND

The yard was fenced to keep horses out,
the wire woven with wild rose, but her house
was built without a lock on the door—
a custom relic from another time;
with a wave of her hand she gave it all
to the people in town at the end.
They came from Athena for the auction,
from Helix, Ione, La Grande—no one
old enough to know her well—
and when the horses, dressed in leather
and brass, were led away, the obsolete
thresher sold, and all the minor glories
of accumulation in an old family,
childless and done, dispersed, they
had to decide about the house,
the oldest in town, magnificent
in its desolation.

It was unsafe, leaning toward the street
from its blooming grove of locust trees.
There was talk of a museum,
'But you can't rebuild the past,'
said the watermelon merchants
to the City Council, and they
were right: 'Preserve what's sound.'
So the Fire Department volunteered
to burn it down—a practice run
to train the men the essentials
of rescue. They'd found
a doll in the attic, wrapped in gingham,

a rude wooden face and hornbeam eyes,
and set it in the round window
niched in the west gable.

Sunday at dawn, without
warning the bell began clanging
and smoke poured from the derelict
cellar and men, dressing as they ran
down Main, clustered at the station
to clamber onto the truck howling
up the hill, the long automatic ladder
already lifting as it entered the yard,
the chief with his ax swaying up through smoke
toward that figure beckoning behind glass.
But then the roof, tinder-dry and shimmering,
blossomed wide; the trees blazed up
in crowns of fire, and the round window
shattered open on a small form dressed in flames.
They pulled the ladder clear, the chief
bundled safe in asbestos boot and glove,
his helmet medalion tarnished by the heat
and eyelashes singed away.

But the children arrived in time
to see that face at the eave, that hand
reach out through a veil of sparks
extending a gift of flame
when the house crumbled into itself
within the rows of burning trees.

HISTORY AT NORTH STAR

The stony field was never farmed
and this town failed—in the hills
its twisted timber never felled, schoolmarm
forked and useless, digger pines reaching
every way but straight. Something
in the heartwood starts the grain
to spiral and lean.

>*the music is ended*
>*the dancing is over*
>*surrender your partner*
>*the moon is gone down*

In her yard the hollow elm is a tunnel
to the sky; a pair of pack rats nest
in the roots, an earring casually left
tarnished at the burrow mouth.

>*the music is ending*
>*the dancers are weary*
>*look to your partner*
>*the moon in your eyes*

The female spider weaves
a spiral of hunger spanning any
opening in the wind—winterkill
branch, doorway without a door.
And the old man breaks
the web unknowing late on a
quiet visit to the empty rooms.

>*the music is ended*
>*the dance nearly over*
>*reach for your partner*
>*the moon goes now*

But the north star never sets,
is always there even at dawn
when it's too light to see.
They said they'd never be back,
yet snow begins billowing
to fill the empty web,
constellation of the moment here
like breath on the frozen pane,
or what the old man sees at the end
of Main—North Star burned in mind.

> *the music is ended*
> *the dancing is over*
> *surrender your partner*
> *the moon is gone down*

BEING THE LAST TO LEAVE

They are locking the doors—
no one else into the world.

How you nurse your glass. Lights
one by one go down, and
the little bells of the money
counted into a bag.

Only those with sons yet living,
only those with daughters yet at home.

You step through the hatch
and it clicks behind, and then
the strange coincidence of rain
on your open hands.

THE FAMILY GATHERED HERE

When a bird sings, someone explains
that it feels good, that this
is how it lives; then others,
more knowing, detect from this
hazel bush to that hawthorn
a territory claimed:
the mating urge is behind it.
And you will observe after midsummer
a stillness in the fields at sunset.

Later, over wine, your musician
friend will identify all bird-song
in a minor key, though we don't
know why, while, beyond the candles,
outside the family gathered here,
at the eave you will see a flicker
of bats, their leather wings
flashing in the moonlight. How they
are like us, says your teacher,
their invisible singing to find each other—
moth, dark tree, stranger, child—
slender hands twitching in their wings.

SLEEPING IN THE BARN

You wake at dawn, snug in the hay.
Warm and steaming, stamping in
through wind the horse comes
storm-weary, eager for oats.
Call this building graceful home:
fog in the field, a wall-board gone,
stall and stanchion long rubbed smooth,
log to post by dovetail tenon,
bale of hay a fragrant table for
tea and bread. Scoop out a
pail of grain from the bin for Rose.
She nibbles the door's old boards.
Invite her in, gently now—
tonight she grazes under the stars.

THE LIGHTHOUSE

You heard about the farm in Dakota
where a single bulb had burned on the porch
for thirty-seven years undimmed,
how people came to look as it burned all day,
all night the landmark on that plain,
went back to their fields to work, to kiss
and sleep, to be born in their homes
all across the land flat as eternity.

They never turned it off,
and children were taught
to walk gently in that house
until they grew and moved away.

There was that light—
then the farm, then Dakota, then winter,
and after dark alone, in pairs or families
the people driving that road would see it
miles away, no matter how late, would make
a little sound under their breath
knowing there was something
other than moonlight
at the core of the human heart.

THE EXODUS

Those who stayed home and survived
say there is first a vacancy;
then the flat windows explode
and everything owned and gone
has the sudden relevance of intoxication:
dishpan, plate and spoon suspended, a box
of water shuddering, as lamp and sofa
hurry past the splintered door.
And just before you black out
clobbered by the bathroom scales in flight
you see all debris dressed in fire
as fragments of your life surrender
to the spiral of the sky.

Here after forty years, we find at dusk
a sacred place in a silent landscape—a sort of
house at the edge of Enid, Oklahoma.
It is unclear, after the long
vandalism of the wind, whether this one
is derelict by a storm, or by the gradual
weathering of the great depression
when the dust bowl bundled our people away.

Come back, we inherit the empty door,
stare on the distant glitter of Enid,
and try to share the moon's patience
with the ruins of American real estate.
Outside, a small, dark angel,
departing with all others, remains
impaled for years on a cactus thorn
where the wind gently stirs
its thin, leather wings.

WEATHERING IN AT WALLOWA

Late in the evening to the water-sound
I walk out from the willows
dressed in snow, where the river
fumbles along with its load of earth
                      and stone.

Uphill from town, above the mill
that burned, the houses glimmering,
in the bluffs is that narrow cave where
children carve their names.

I crawl inside, turn to look.
Back down the tunnel framed by stone
a patch of town flickers
beyond a veil of snow.

I go down in the dark
toward the patch of town,
devoted to what I see–a distant
window tapered like a star.

THE MESSENGERS

I

Alone during a storm
in a cave on an island
you can carry a lantern
half a mile into the mountain,
sometimes bowing down, and once
for seven paces on your knees.
At the end, like learning to sleep
again, you put out the light and reach
toward the wall you remember
in the disbelief of absolute darkness
and stare until the hand itself
blooms forth, begins to see.

II

North of the Brooks Range
in the ornithologists' cabin
abandoned when they began to starve
is a short library for the wilderness:
a book on weather, one on birds,
the history of stone, a manual
of the stars on the shelf
split from tamarack and sagging
above the bear-proof door.
They had to listen a long time
to hear the edge of winter
over the blue horizon of darkness.

III

Slender over the water at Elwha
is a woman made of madrone
who bent to see her face
and never straightened, never
walked away to rejoin the others.

The way a tree goes down on its knees
to crawl toward light
she goes down and reaches,
swaying out and out.
I stand in the water,
my hand on a branch, smooth
as a wrist of wind.

IV

Limb by limb in November
I pruned the straggling pear,
took down a mound of wood
and meant to burn it in July.
But in April, before
the old tree woke, that pile
of twigs exploded into bloom
and the bees went wild–
no root or leaf, no chance
of fruit or long life, only
the sweet extravagance
of being alive.

V

Arriving late at the river
helpless with sleep between the trees
we watch the moon, old connoisseur
of silence sliding through the storm.
We gather against a log of cedar
the river left hollow behind.
What happens is strongest.
Together on a dark road
we could set out, armed only
with a loaf of bread
and the kind of news that takes
many tellings in the storm.

MORIZIA

(after the Rumanian ballad)

Cars go gleaming on the road,
a ragged man with his staff
walking by the way. Rush hour
and evenings darkens. He listens
for the light clatter of rain
and stone. The cars plod easy
toward the fold.

'Old shepherd, do not go alone
this night to your bed on the hill.
Two men travel far and cold
through the rain to take your life
because you are weak and it is dark.'

'It is dark but tell them not to weep.
We are an individual, earth and I.
Tell my mother to dress me in white;
there is one in a crown of stars,
a coat of darkness. Her days are
by the moon. She kindles my heart,
she guides me apart with her slender hand.'

SALAMANDER

No doctor, no lover
can make a creature live—
only help its own desire
to breathe, to speak, or need
to speak, after its own kind, which is
this salamander's forefoot raised
in my hand, amphibian gesture
eloquent, futile as a falling leaf.
And so the beginning, the seed
I carry no physician, friend or
dreamer ever could restore, so
fragile is desire.
                Transparent
amphibians breathe through skin, gently
tugging at the world pore by pore,
delicate as the eye blinking. My hand
dry as fire, I bow to earth, return
the salamander there, its little
palm still raised, luminous
under wet leaves.

CARPENTER

This is a plain profession–
as the trees put on wood
layer by layer, ring by ring,
so I with patience and respect
will take the tree apart
shaving after shaving,
the blade of the plane
sliding through centuries.
Then the ring and whisper
of the saw, the ping
of 16d nails driven home.
And when the sill, stud,
header, plate stand complete,
the sheathing on, the window
in, I lay the plane
down, on its side, to rest.
This is the best work–to build
a kind of human hollow tree
and call it home.

THE BEARS

My brother saw the amorous bear
rolling about in the meadow up by
Louder Mountain–the lupine crushed,
the paintbrush flattened in their
loving swathe–how he nibbled
her ear and she smacked him
with her paw, there in the fall
of fat September. And my brother
crept away on hands and knees
into the hemlock thicket.
Then the rain, the snow, and we
in our separate lives content
because sunlight struck a pair
apart from our human way,
the wearing of shoes, and words,
and nations.

MR. EPP'S GARDEN IN AURORA

Find a railway dining car, made into a home,
parked forever, at the heart of Aurora,
and a bay horse, one leg raised, asleep
tethered to the rail. If you follow
the road from there, you'll find
the garden open dawn to dusk in the care
of a Mr. Epp, who's out of town today,
so you'll not hear the names
ripple from his mouth–pennyroyal,
mother of thousands, mother of thyme.

On a kind of yarrow, witness a spider,
the precise pollen-canary of its chosen flower,
drawing nectar from a bee, as the bee itself
drew from the flower, and the flower
from the rain.

At dusk, drive north toward the city
on old 99. You'll meet the sign
for a town that failed and holds,
like Aurora, to its name: New Era,
all moss and fern.
Here comes the rain.

THE SURFACE

Deeply forgetful,
happy with small things
you stand here still.
Luminous on the floor, a rare day
in February scatters the small debris
at the closing door:
wisp and sliver by the stove,
shred of cedarbark, sawdust
crumb, in the hall flecks
of bran glimmering like gnats' wings,
or the far lights of a city
across the bay, in the doorway
your lover's hair, red strand compliant,
powerful as the tide that wrinkles
the brink of deep water, or that
slow shadow wind makes at dusk
moving like a river through fields.
Then, by the glint from a small crescent
of fingernail, the young moon rises
distant over a meadow of lint.

MY OUTERMOST FACE

This is a place where nothing
happens, so I am here.
I move across the square
like leaf. Yesterday they
held me; today wind
is my friend. The afternoon
breeze takes me apart.
I roll, then lie flat.
Rain penetrates my face–
I had my day.

Father was blind,
mother the stand he stood by
all day, jingling coins;
his hand reached closer
until evening. He gave
me away. I was colder.
Wet palms spread me wide–
I have never been young
since then.

I speak now
from a dark place.
It is night. My outermost
face has found a cave,
a space its size.
I am grown so thin, my voice
become a single crumple.
Do you hear, you
who need so much
a withered friend like me?

NO PORT BUT PASSAGE

When the iceberg first is seen
miles ahead, it seems the ship
lies still, and that the ice,
looming up like a thing remembered,
bears toward our bow.
The cabin boy wakes the captain;
they turn a wheel. The ship
stirs, grazed below the water-line:
all silent, all calm.

In every darkened compartment
the crew sleeps, the passengers
wakeful, hungry for the new land.
An old man leans at the rail, three
sisters walk by dark, hand to hand,
and a couple in their cabin say over
and again, 'I will, we will, God's will.'
By their bed a child sleeps
in an open suitcase.

A bell is rung, a voice, muffled
by fog, cries out, a door
clangs closed, distant, then
another, another, down the tunnel
of the hold. In a dim room
a ring of listeners turned outward—
the great engines gone still,
the ship gliding on, slightly
listing to starboard.

The hull of ice slips away astern
toward its rendezvous with dissolution.
And still it seems we could
never go down—no wind,
the same small waves, the deck
beneath us firm, steady as
she goes. Within, woman and man
begin a dance, the child
glimmering at their feet.

When the lights go out, the lifeboats,
too few, are lowered to the waves.
Below, at the throb of water,
the pressured ping of steel,
the ship's designer fingers
a map of the world, and will refuse,
like many, to join the boats.
The orchestra plays, the men
shout, the women begin to row.

Slowly, the stern rises up;
the ship descends into the sea:
a shattered cry from the emigrants
going down by blue light, slipping
into the cold. The cabin boy and the
captain turn like a single wheel.
The dancers sway through the deep,
a sentence bubbling from her mouth,
his embrace first hard, then gentle.

My hand, jerked down, melts
from the rail. I whirl,
dumbfounded by the plunge,
the torque of water wringing
syllables from my lungs, my hands
climbing through a flock of chairs,
a pounding in my ears, arms
slowed, heavy by the cold
and then the air, sharp, rich.

When the rescue boats arrive, voices
flicker from the cluttered waves. Overhead
before dawn a flare opens, and they
find in the bright, luxurious debris
a man adrift clinging to a cello, two
sisters bundled on a plank of ice,
a steamer trunk rocking in the wreckage
with a child inside.

Numb, inarticulate, we are lifted
from the waves, wrapped in new clothing,
revived with tea. I tell this tale,
already vague as fog: a bell,
a few words, a pounding within,
and a sudden, desperate patience
filling my body when I shook
through the surface, broke open
my mouth, and was born.

DAWN OF THE MOON

Come this way, through salal,
lush with dew, heavy with berries;
some are ripe, soft in your fingers—
crush one at your tongue.
Wave to a friend like this—
white rag of the hand flutters
(save this gesture for September
right at dark in the rain).
Shut the door, light the candle now;
hear the surf out there, slow
but steady like a heart—
clear enough, close enough?
Soon it will bury your steps.
Moonrise. Pinch out the flame.

A LESSON IN ARCHITECTURE

The design of the fingerprint is to hold
everything smooth, the design of water
to make graceful all it can touch, and
we meet here, the quince leaf in hand
in the rain. The old tree sags
in September, a knobbed branch sways,
as leaves and fruit keep a fragile hold
to wood. A thorned vine of blackberry
spirals into the trunk's dark hollow
to root. Under the arch of a limb I bow
over the leaf in hand to find
vein by vein the cause and design
of all the eye can touch, the cave
of a dying tree, the doorway of light
tattered with glistening leaves.
And here inside is home,
the graceful ruin of the world.

LETTER TO PHIL

There may be a hoofprint or two out
there yet, frozen in the meadow ground,
filling with snow, your gloves by the
splitting maul, the aspen grove you
looked at so long worn smooth by it all.
That reminds me of the song or saying,
'You are my burden, you are my strength.'

Moonlit nights you'd appear at the woodpile
in a white robe and slippers. Ax would flash,
snow fly, and any log gleam open at your feet:
ninety years' growth.

'Pleasant words are as a honeycomb—
sweet to the soul, health to the bones,'
and there you were, stomping snow off your boots
till the rafters shook. That night you sang
and paused, and we heard coyotes out across
the meadow linger on a name. A mile or so
of wind went by before you sang again. That's
what spooks horses and cures thieves—
the silence all gone extra deep.

TWENTY-EIGHT

I

Alone, I look out at the light.
Beyond the window a loon
alert on the water goes under.
With the clear sun I follow.

Down there, in the long furrow,
the dark form soars:
it is a gentle compliment
to be born, to be alive at all–

you deserve the world,
you are strong and ready.
The loon emerges, flies off,
a graceful movement in the light.

II

On the island at the center of sleep
I find the people I know–names
on the tongue sweet as water–
at every stage of fortune, exile,

age, and discovery, gathered
here by fog and candlelight within
the dim room behind my eyes,
all turning in a ring.

I learn to move to the rhythm
of the waves, then wake, assured:
no one is going to change it.
Together we'll grow old.

CADILLAC

We kept a rabbit named for a car
and a car named for an old woman
while the old woman down the road
kept thirty horses under the cedar trees.
We gave her squash, she gave us manure;
the squash grew thick, honeybees
staggering from the blossom tongues,
pollen-covered and a little drunk.
The rabbit sprawled white and drowsy
in the dusky light of the grass,
and the year passed flower
to flower.
          Trees grew close
together, the blossoms closed by dark.
All things were fragile with us then.
On the shaggy trunk we loved
there was a wound in the wood
that bark closed over and concealed.

FOR PRINTERS & TRAVELERS

It's all rain to the river now;
the journey's over. You've made
a faint impression on the world, the long
chain of footprints where wind comes
sniffing along the trail, and the leaves
all piled on a stone.

When it's done, sort things out
letter by letter to the snug little rooms
of the job-case, that pathless labyrinth
of the shallow drawer memorized–
slender corridors for 'l' and 'f,'
arena for 'e.' All things to be said

are here, all things said
already, all things forgotten,
waiting again: the night of
three-thousand folds, pair of hands
as if dipped in cream, and a book
goes out shuffled with light.

As if you never came here the chair
is vacant, long bed of the press
clear and the rollers clean,
furniture stacked in place,
en-quad, ampersand chambered
in the honeycomb where they belong.

All things have an address and a name,
all things are useful, all things are
justified by work, all things worn
in meeting. Old friends, retire
to your rooms, the drawer slid home.
It's all rain to the river now.

IT BEGINS WITH ASHES

The wind, a bag of names,
sifts through the spangled fruit
of earth. A place of rest,
a happening, a way of opening
occurs: man is wakened,
woman unlocked, the child
buds within. And within the child
the soft bones form, dew hardens,
a skeleton of fog limber and contained
retreats from change into a shape.

First the ripple of flame,
then it begins.

A wave's poise is held awhile.
Through it all things flow,
flourish and depart: in spring
the rehearsal of the petal-fall
so that each tree may know
about leaves. Then the body
is retrieved from the actual world,
the shape of a life submerged
hollow in stone, the damp softening
even of bone, and the wind
harvesting several bruised apples
into a pouch of light.

WAITING TO BE BORN

Check that blue against
the darkness of the names.
　　　　　　–printer's remark

You could hesitate forever, waiting
to be born, patiently to find a use
for pale, thin leather, for eyes,
for hair or feathers (you could decide
slowly, your time worth nothing).

And they do well without you now,
there in the water, in every
ripple of the rose petal, the
window of a pair of wings.
They are patient too.

But here, before it begins,
you will forget the names
for *luna, Deo,* honeybee–
they come later, with a voice.
Here, you hardly have to do
with sound, with flicker of fin
or finger. They come later,
when they are useful.

Now, in the lamp of water,
you undress in darkness–
with a flash the fabric leaves you.

Carnegie-Mellon Poetry

1975
The Living and the Dead, Ann Hayes
In the Face of Descent, T. Alan Broughton

1976
The Week the Dirigible Came, Jay Meek
Full of Lust and Good Usage, Stephen Dunn

1977
*How I Escaped from the Labyrinth and
    Other Poems*, Philip Dacey
The Lady from the Dark Green Hills, Jim Hall
For Luck: Poems 1962-1977, H.L. Van Brunt
By the Wreckmaster's Cottage, Paula Rankin

1978
New & Selected Poems, James Bertolino
The Sun Fetcher, Michael Dennis Browne
A Circus of Needs, Stephen Dunn
The Crowd Inside, Elizabeth Libbey

1979
Paying Back the Sea, Philip Dow
Swimmer in the Rain, Robert Wallace
Far From Home, T. Alan Broughton
The Room Where Summer Ends, Peter Cooley
No Ordinary World, Mekeel McBride

1980
*And the Man Who Was Traveling Never Got
    Home*, H.L. Van Brunt
Drawing on the Walls, Jay Meek
The Yellow House on the Corner, Rita Dove
The 8-Step Grapevine, Dara Wier
The Mating Reflex, Jim Hall

1981
A Little Faith, John Skoyles
Augers, Paula Rankin
Walking Home from the Icehouse, Vern Rutsala
Work and Love, Stephen Dunn
The Rote Walker, Mark Jarman
Morocco Journal, Richard Harteis
Songs of a Returning Soul, Elizabeth Libbey

1982
The Granary, Kim R. Stafford
Calling the Dead, C.G. Hanzlicek